Life With Maud

For my family and loved ones

Ken Hughes 2024

Life With Maud

Index

Life with Maud

War and Peace

There was a sadness, something behind the eyes. As though he'd experienced something that he couldn't talk about. The way he dealt with it was to laugh. A big laugh, a raucous laugh. It would burst out of him at the drop of a hat and catch you up in its enthusiasm. You wanted to be a part of it, whatever it was. You wanted to play.

It never changed, from when he was a ten-year old boy to a fifty-year-old man. The sadness was harder to spot. There was just a hint of it in the eyes. The sadness and the lust for life lived in him side by side. Sometimes you might see a glimpses of it, but mainly just the broadcasts of joy.

He was my half- brother. He was my father's son. His mother had died when a bomb dropped on their house at the end of the Second World War. He and my father were dug out of the wreckage. They survived. I never ever saw a photograph of his mother. She was never mentioned or talked about at all. We were a family of story tellers, so it was odd.

I wonder now if he ever knew her. Did he remember her? Did he miss her? He was still only a baby when my father met my mother and my sister, June, who was about 12 years old then. They were neighbors in 'Nissen hutted' temporary accommodation. They had both been blown out of their homes. Both victims. Shaken and stirred but still standing.

My mother used to baby sit for my father. One day close to Christmas she took Geoff back to him and something unexpected happened. He kissed her under the mistletoe hanging above the front door. She went weak at the knees. "It was like an electric current went through me Ken", she would tell me time and time again over the years. I never tired of hearing the story or seeing the far-away look in her eyes. It was as though she was experiencing it all over again. I spent most of my adult life looking for the same thing to happen to me. I wanted that moment of magic too. That certainty that you were meant to be. Whatever happened, it was meant to be. And things did happen.

I didn't arrive until 1949. By then they had married and set up a new home. My mother, my father, my brother Geoff and my sister June. A new post war house with a garden, a gate that led into the woods the meadows and the river beyond. It was idyllic just the thing after all the chaos and turmoil of war. A shed for my father, and a garden for them both. Then I came along, unexpected, a surprise, a gift. Perfect.

It was certainly perfect for me They all loved me. I was unaware of what loss and trauma was being coped with. Or the tension or sadness below the surface of the smiles?

It wasn't hard for me to be oblivious. All those endless days in the woods at the back of the house. Laying in the long grass, looking at the clouds and the sky. Feeling the sun on my face and the damp of the earth below me, becoming a part of me. Adrift on a safe eternal sea, my mother's voice calling me home for tea.

Then, one day, when I was about six years old it happened. The fear got loose. My mother wasn't smiling, patting my head and checking the buttoned- down top pocket of my shirt for hidden beetles. She was distracted, crying and holding me tight. Just crying and crying. She couldn't stop. She held me close, she sobbed and said "Oh Ken, I'm so frightened". I froze, the fear passed into me, and filled me up.

She didn't get better. It didn't go away like I hoped. She became paralyzed with fear. We didn't know what to do or what to say. My father was mortified. Desperately calm but hopelessly lost. One day the doctor came with the sad eyes and the soft voice. They took her away in an ambulance. My father at the door. "Don't let them take me away Jim", she pleaded as they took her away. I stood at the back of the hall looking on, terrified that she would never come back.

But she did come back, after a while. After the electric shock treatments. The visits to the strange hospitals where she sat in a dinghy threadbare lounge, calmer and quiet. Not crying anymore but still lost somehow.

Eventually she came back home. She was bright and shiny and brand new. Kissing and hugging and telling me how much she loved me. How she would make it all up to me and never leave me again. The fear in me subsided and the sun came out again.

There were more bright happy days and safe nights. Until it happened all over again. It would happen every year for 4 or 5 years until they found the right medication for her. She suffered these spells of depression, for the rest of her adult life. In time and with the right medication it became more of a passing storm that was manageable. Not the absolute despair and complete beak down of the past.

The strange thing is I can't remember my brother Geoff or my sister June through any of this. It's as though they disappeared. I was so consumed by her despair and my fear that other people became invisible. Even my father is just a kind of half ghost in the kitchen, cooking omelets and making Victoria sponge cakes. His good but limited repertoire.

My brother Geoff was there though, and he taught me a lot. Not how to cope with all of that. None of us had a clue how to cope with all of that. But in 'normal times' he taught me what not to do. He rushed in and I stood by and watched and weighed it up.

One of my first lessons began in Woolworths in the local High Street when I was only about 5 years old. He wanted the tin drum with the yellow cord strap and the two wooden drumsticks. "You can't have the drum", my mother said in that matter of fact, no nonsense, nothing more to be said way that she had. But Geoff persisted and got louder and more fraught. Her face tightened around the mouth. Oh dear, I thought, this is a mistake. He didn't stop though, he laid on the floor and cried and kicked. In public too. That just wasn't done. Then she said in a gruff whisper, "Stop it Geoffrey, I'll get the drum". Blimey, I thought, it does work after all.

We walked back home from the High Street with our neighbor, Mrs. Parsons and her daughter Jill. Geoff was clutching his prize, wrapped up with brown paper and sellotape. My mother was tight-lipped and Mrs. Parsons said, "Don't worry Maud they all get like that sometimes". When I heard my mother's terse response of "Do they?", I could sense it wasn't over.

We said goodbye to Mrs. Parsons and Jill and followed my mother through the back door into the green and cream kitchen. We'd hardly entered the room, still had our coats on. Geoff was clutching the parcel happy and oblivious. She turned to face us, stern and serious. Her suppressed fury seemed to make her bigger, she filled the room up as she glared at us, but thankfully mainly at Geoff. "Give me the drum, Geoffrey", she said, and he handed it over. She took the drum and carefully placed it on the linoleum floor. She looked straight at us with those furious eyes and then jumped up and down on the drum until it was squashed flat. We were stunned, mouths hanging open. She said, "If you ever do that again it won't be the drum it will be you".

I think Geoff was too shocked to cry. I stood there thinking thank God I didn't ask for the trumpet.

There were other days and other lessons, of course. She was a complicated woman. I became aware that the relationships between men and women were complicated too and could be difficult to fully grasp. Not just me but for my father too.

I was standing next to her in the kitchen looking out of the window into the garden. My father was carrying a cardboard box down the path. The cardboard box had six kittens in it. We'd lost 'Mickey' the cat for a few days. Then we found, up until then..., what we'd thought of as 'him', in the cupboard under the sink. He /she had given birth to a litter of kittens. After the collected astonishment had died down, my mother went into a negative spiral about it.

What were we going to do with them. We couldn't afford to keep them. Where would we put them. Who would look after them etc?

"We'll give them away or sell them," my father said positively, "No one will want them", she scoffed. No matter how positive he tried to be she shot him down. I realised something else was going on here. She was goading him. How was he going to solve this problem and prove himself. We were standing in the kitchen looking at the huddle of kitten, but the air was charged with something else.
Then he said it, "Well I'll just have to get rid of them?".
She was in like a three- sided knife, "What do you mean, get rid of them". How would you get rid of them?"

"I'd drown them," he said unconvincingly.
"Where would you drown them?" she said.
"Don't be daft Jim".
"In the well" he said, "at the bottom of the garden".
"You couldn't drown them" she scoffed. "Let's face it we're stuck with them." She looked straight at him. The ball was absolutely in his court.

"Oh yes I can" he bristled, "if that's what we've got to do then that's what we've got to do. So I may as well do it now, the sooner the better."
He strode out of the back door and came back

with a cardboard box, gently put the mewing kittens in it, picked up the box, faced my mother and said "Right that's it then".

"You aren't going to drown them Jim," she said, "you haven't got it in you".
"Well, that's where your wrong", he said and turned and went out the back door. We stood there looking out of the kitchen window as he walked down the path to the well clutching the box of kittens. Then she said, very quietly and more to herself than me. "If he drowns those kittens I'll never speak to him again" I was amazed and confused!!

We stood there for a while in complete silence until finally he came back up the garden path, still clutching the box, his head down, his tread heavy. I held my breath.
He came in through the back door. We could see the kittens were still in the box. He looked up at my mother and said, "I couldn't do it Maud, they looked at me and I couldn't do it".

"Oh well, never mind" she said, "we'll sort something out."
She turned to me and her eyes said, "see, this is why we love him'.

I haven't a clue what did happen to the kittens, I can't remember playing with them or who had them in the end. Everything else about it is completely obliterated by the emotional super nova of this encounter.

She was never predictable.

There were times many years later, when mum and I weren't getting on. I was 15 and wanting to find my own way. I had my own mind and views. I didn't like being told what to do. I still don't.
I was a teenager. Sometimes we would clash. I can see now I am a bit like her, but would never have seen that back then

It was a Sunday night. We were watching TV together. I was probably bored stiff. There was Liberace on the TV he was sitting at his piano, there was an ornate telephone on the piano lid. The telephone rang. He picked it up, mugged at the audience and said "gee it's my mom" "See"" said my mother. "He loves his mother. You could take a leaf out of his book" "Of course it's not his bloody mother" I spluttered back.
"Jim, are you going to let him talk to me like that?"

And we were off…..Happy days

Home Improvements

Of course, there were ordinary days.
Days that drifted one into the other.
Calm days, giving our life together some
ballast, so we didn't turn over and
capsize.

Days in the constantly green and cream
kitchen. Days when the radio was always
on. 'Worker's playtime' at lunch time.
'Woman's hour' and 'listen with mother'
in the afternoon, 'Listen with Mother'
even the name sounds safe and cosy.
Every evening my mother cooking my
father's tea then disappearing upstairs to
put on a clean dress, a bit of lipstick and
a quick squirt of scent. Reappearing just
as the 'Archers' theme would start up on
the radio. "Dum de dum de dum de
dum".
We would hear my father's key turn in
the front door. He would walk in. She
would turn from the stove and smile.
"Hello Jim, your dinner's nearly ready". It
was like an advert for the perfect family.
I loved it.

These were the safe, happy days, that
we all clung to. Yet, after a while we had
to escape from. We had to play, just a
little bit.

One of their pleasures was the garden. My mother knelt attentive in the flower beds. My father watering and unable to resist spraying her, just A BIT, in passing. "Don't Jim", she would say in a firm but pleasant tone. Of course he had to do it again. Eventually, after she'd half- filled a bucket with water and chucked it over him. She'd be screaming and running round the garden. Him chasing her with the hose, both absolutely saturated. Me delighted.

There were also home improvements. It wasn't called DIY in those days. My father could turn his hand to anything and do it well. His shed was his domain. It was a temple of quiet purpose. Everything had a place, there was a place for everything. Every tool valued, aged with careful handling and being put to good use.

There was a calmness there. There was a calmness in my father as he focussed on the task. There was a magic in the sleeping lathe that seemed so complex to operate. The foot pedal operated fret saw that he used with such easy skill. I would just stand there and watch him. I'd take in the smell of the oil and the wood and sawdust. I never took in any of the skills or techniques. I was so enrapt with the experience that I didn't learn anything useful. Not dove-tail joint kind useful anyway.

It was a place where he could escape from the feeling of hopelessness in the face of the black depression that would take over my mother. He could do nothing about that despite his love for her. In the shed he was master of the universe. A benign dictator. Nothing happened without his say so. Plans were made and brought to fruition. He called the tune and hit every nail home, perfect and true.

He also turned his hand to decoration which was more quixotic. Driven partly by economy and partly by creativity. He would distemper the walls blue and paint clouds on them at high level. Then he would paint scenes on the back of old wallpapers, cut them out and paste them on the walls, with the blue sky and clouds as a backdrop.

The rooms had themes. In the front room he recreated the garden, around the walls. The sundial, the well, his shed, the dog 'Rex', sitting on the path. The unused door into the hall painted up to look like a window looking out into the garden. It was great.

The dining room had scenes from 'Dickens' with horse drawn coaches. With smiling men in stove pipe hats, smoking long curly pipes. All amiably mingling on our walls.

The bathroom, had mermaids, pirates and a tropical island. At the time didn't seem at all odd to me that no one else we knew had mermaids in the loo.
My mother occasionally ventured into the decorative arena. It was inevitably more bizarre. She would, every now and then be taken up with the urge to paint. She would raid my fathers shed and get all the paint pots left over. Not one of them. All of them. She would then proceed to paint the rockery in the front garden with a dab of paint from each pot. It looked like multi-coloured measles. She was always delighted with it and could never be talked out of it. Oddly enough people seemed to like it. An unexpected splash of colour in an otherwise dull world. A bit like her.

It did develop this rockery obsession. By

the time I was fifteen I was working in 'Pricerites', a local supermarket. 'Omo' washing powder had a promotion where you were given a free, cheap and nasty, plastic tulip or daffodil with each purchase. When the promotion ended, I made the mistake of telling my mother that there were quite a few boxes of plastic flowers left over in the warehouse. Her eyes lit up. You could see gears turning in that unfathomable brain. A Maud type plan was taking shape. She was up the High Street in a flash. In no time at all she had charmed the manager into letting her have all the remaining plastic tulips and plastic daffodils. We are talking 50 to 60 plastic tulips and daffodils. "What are you going to do with them"? we asked tentatively. "Just you wait and see", she said. "Just you wait and see".

I came home from school the next evening and was stunned to find the plastic flowers planted in the rockery. In the front garden too. Not the back garden. The front garden, that faced onto the street and was open to view and to ridicule. There was no moving her. We should have known. The more we tried, the more fun it was. The more her determination set in. To my surprise, people liked it. Well, some people liked it. Occasionally someone knocked on the door in Winter with two inches of snow on the ground said, "Your flowers are doing well aren't they?". I tried through my silence to adopt a detachment to it, hoping that people would see it as a sort of surreal joke. A statement about the absurdity of suburbia. Perhaps, it was.

Games

My mother wasn't an easy woman. She was complicated and clever. There was a raw intelligence in her. She'd had a basic Victorian education as a girl and had excelled at being a bit of a rebel. It was in her nature. But it didn't help that her father was away in the Navy in the First World War during her formative years. Only to return home, a stranger to her and someone who turned her out of her mother's bed. She didn't like it and she didn't like him much either.
A battle of wills commenced. She was stubborn. He was stubborn. I'm stubborn, and so it goes.

I don't know what she was taught at school, but I do know one things she learnt. "Never, ever put up with bullies Ken", she would often tell me. She was heartfelt about not suffering bullies. Whoever they were, young, old, bigger than you, more important. It didn't matter, they were to be challenged and resisted.

I believed her totally. I took it on. It got me into trouble sometimes, but I rarely waivered. I always remembered her conviction. Although it probably wasn't in the forefront of my mind, when I collapsed to the ground in the school playground, after the kick in the bollocks I'd received from the hulking fifth former. He was two years older and twice my size. I'd stupidly answered back, after he'd pushed me in the chest and demanded I get his football back for him. The only thought in my mind at that moment of searing pain was 'mistake'.

She was incredibly bright. But you didn't need all that wit and energy just to bring up a couple of children and make good steak and kidney pies. Perhaps that was part of her problem. She had this unspent energy and desire. It could make her brilliant, beautifully spontaneous, and gloriously generous. Or it could turn to mischief. "Idle hands make the devil's work", she would often say. And it did.

It would turn her frustrated and scheming. Arguments, and falling outs. Soap operas would be constructed from just the wrong response, a perceived slight, or just a fantasy that she created out of her unhappiness. These soap operas could last for days or weeks. In the case of some of the neighbors, for years. One day they were using our mangle and the next day we were forbidden to talk to them. It was beyond me, and I'm sure they were perplexed. Or the energy would turn in on her and consume her until all that was left was the void and the fear. That was the worst.

There was no middle ground with her at all. It was either summer or winter. The sun was out and she was cart wheeling across the sand with a grin. Or it was dark and cold and she was withdrawing into herself.

She was brave though. She had courage. She had the nerve to play with people, and to entertain. When the going was good.

She would mimic a neighbor's whiney voices when we bumped into her in the street. As she moaned about her husband, and I stood silently beside her. She'd look down at me and wink as she got away with it. She would gleefully stuff her shopping bag up her coat in order to look heavily pregnant. Then step off the pavement to bring the traffic to a sudden halt, or to get a seat offered on the bus. She would deliberately knock someone's hat off with the rose bush we'd just bought at the market. She'd then go into an elaborate pantomime of apology. She was street theatre.

She would insist on bargaining with the man in the local paper shop. "That's a newspaper and ten weights, that'll be fourteen and six Maud". "I'll give you thirteen and six", she'd say. "No Maud, I can't take thirteen and six, it's fourteen and six and that's it".. "Well, I'm only giving you thirteen and six so take it or leave it".
And he'd take it.

She would dance around in the new supermarket with the piped music, to my embarrassment. But they loved it and they loved her.

Yes, she had courage. She had the courage to return. To come back from all those nervous breakdowns. From the shock treatments, and the drugs. Time and time again. She fought the same battle every year. That's real courage.

She was an entertainer. Sometimes comedy and sometimes tragedy. We had an 'Ace' record player that you could stack ten vinyl singles on. They would automatically drop down and play, one on top of the other. Forget stereo clarity and a clean sound, we just needed the noise. There were times when it was always on. She had songs that she would become obsessed with. They'd always be playing. She would learn all the words and sing along. Or more worryingly, she'd go into a semi trance like state, eyes unfocussed. Silently mouthing the words.

They would normally be high on drama songs full of big passions.

The highs, but more likely the lows. The loss, the despair. 'it's All in the Game' by Tommy Edwards, "many a tear has to fall, but it's all in the game….", she loved it and knew every word. There were others,' I who have nothing' by Shirley Bassey, 'Make the world go away' Jim Reeves and so on.

There was occasionally the odd cuckoo in the musical nest. Like 'Don't bring Lulu', which was an up-tempo ragtime song from 'Thoroughly Modern Milly'. It was all bright and kooky and although a bit of a relief from all the tears falling. It was almost too bright. As tended to bring out the kooky side of my mother. She would grin wildly when this was on and swing her artificial pearls about. It was a tough call really.

She got immense pleasure out of it. These songs, all this music. And I can see now that I've inherited this from her. I hated her bloody records at the time. I mean 'It's all in the game' is quite a good song. But after two hundred spins on the 'Ace' turntable I bloody hated it. I could sing you all the words through and to 'Don't bring Lulu'. But it wasn't so much the songs, it was the depth of her rapture. That's what infected me.

Sometimes she was so taken up with a song that she'd have to perform it. One day I came home from school, I was about twelve or thirteen years old. She was super charming. "What would you like for tea, Ken?". "Sit down, leave your homework for a bit, cup of tea?". Once she'd got me settled, trapped at the kitchen table, then she sprang it on me.

"I've been working on this song, Ken, I wondered what you might think of it?". Oh, no, I thought, how embarrassing she's going to sing to me. Well, she didn't just sing to me, she performed it. It was much worse and yet ….
Impressive.

We had a pair of heavy curtains separating the opening between the kitchen and the dining room. No doors, just curtains. She went through the curtains into the dining room. Then she announced herself from behind the curtain. "Ladies and gentlemen, we are proud to present Maud Ivy Hughes, who is going to sing for you her latest top ten hit 'My Way'. Please give her a big round of applause". She burst through the curtain as I clapped twice, confused and startled. She launched into the song and sang it with every fibre of her being. Arms flung wide, clutching her heart. Eyes fixed on some distant imaginary spotlight, that was somewhere past the back door and in the coal shed.

She sang the song and she wrung it dry. I was embarrassed, my cheeks were red. I was embarrassed because I didn't know how to be. Not because she sang it badly, but because it was so passionate. The song, the emotions and the performance were too big for the kitchen. It filled the room up. She filled the room up. I was breathless.

Many years later when she was in her eighties, I would go and visit her in her warden-controlled bungalow. Things were slightly different then. It would be me who would start singing. She would mention something in conversation like, "Geoff was in the Navy for quite a few years" and that would be enough to trigger me off. "All the nice girls love a sailor," I'd sing at the top of my voice. She would immediately join in. She loved it and the afternoon conversations would be peppered with bursts of song. When she started going along to the Salvation Army, we'd sit in her tiny living room and sing hymns from the Sally Army songbook. She particularly liked the upbeat dramatic ones, like 'Onward Christian Soldiers'. She would access the passion that I had seen in the kitchen that day.

My father must have absolutely loved her. He must have done. I never ever once, in all those years and sometimes very difficult times, ever heard him run her down or complain about her. There was never any doubt that he would stand by her, and he did. He made the most of it too. When her sun was out, he would encourage her to play and fan the flame of her lust for life.

There was the hot Sunday afternoon in August after lunch. My mother and father washing up at the sink. My brother and I still sat at the table. Sunday in the suburbs. A kind of resigned exhaustion everywhere. All the windows of the houses wide open, desperate for a breeze. The sound of distant radio. The low mumble of a distant conversation. A child being scolded. All the same. Safe, still, stupefying.

"I'm bored Jim", my mother said, still washing dishes. "Let's have an argument" my father said, without the slightest hesitation. Her eyes brightened and her chin lifted. She understood immediately. It was time to play. "You move a bit further away, "he said, positioning her like on a stage set. Then he opened the windows wide. "Oh, wait a minute". He grabbed a chair and enthusiastically dug out some old plates from a high-level cupboard and rushed back. She grinned, Geoff and were perplexed.

Then they started. "I've just about had enough", he bellowed at the top of his voice, so that it carried out into the air and into all the other open windows.

"Every week it's the same bloody thing".
"It's alright for you to talk", she shouted
back. "You think I'm just some sort of
scivvy, just here to clean up after you".
Geoff and I slumped in embarrassment.
"Well, you've got another thing coming",
she yelled, "I'm up to here with it all".
At this point he casually tossed a plate
out of the open window which smashed
noisily on the concrete paving. Then he
handed her a plate.

The silence that followed was palpable.
Radios were turned off. There were no
distant voices. You could sense the
neighbors, straining like deer, to catch all
of this. Now they were sure they'd got
everyone's attention, he carried on.
"Now look what you've done he said,
typical, money doesn't grow on trees".
She tossed the next plate. "Don't talk to
me about money", smash, "that's all you
think about, …………", smash.
"Well it's fine for you to talk you don't
have to get the train to work every day
do you ….." smash.   "Just bloody swan
about here all day complaining ……."
smash. It went on until they ran out of
old plates and steam.
It was somehow more embarrassing to
me and Geoff because it was a game.
People would think they were mad.

I look back now and absolutely love it.

Christmas

Christmases were sometimes strange affairs. In so many ways it was perfect. Particularly Christmas Eve. The house beautifully decorated by dad. Rudolph the Red Nosed Reindeer on the radio. My mother in her pinny, covered with a light dusting of flour, singing in the kitchen. Busy making mince pies and sausage rolls, that you touched on pain of death on Christmas Eve, when they were hot and the house was full of the smell of them. Then were forced to eat on Christmas day or Boxing Day, when they had gone cold, and you were so full of turkey you thought you might burst.

It all started so well. Full of bright happy music, wonderful smells and smiling faces. Full of anticipation. But by Boxing Day afternoon it was all over. We were fading. Full up and slightly bored.
As the sausage rolls cooled, so did we. Bertram Mills circus on the television failed to lift our spirits. Even when my Grand Mother (who only ever left her flat and came to our house at Christmas), insisted that the performing animals, even the lions, were not real animals. They were men dressed up in animal suits. It just made us more unsettled.

It was on a day like this that my brother Geoff impressed me the most. On this particular Boxing Day, he was magnificent. We were slumped in front of the TV. Gripped in a fog of lethargy. I was about thirteen, Geoff was twenty/twenty- one, and on leave from the Royal Navy. No doubt Sidcup seemed a bit tame after Singapore.

My mother had been quietly nagging my father for about twenty minutes. Just trying to provoke an argument. It was boredom making her edgy and up for trouble. Dad, being dad, wasn't rising to the bait. We all just sat there suffering this low-key grumbling. Suddenly, Geoff leapt to his, feet roaring like a lion. He reached out for the nearest object. This happened to be the solid brass Chinese temple dog that we used as a door stop. It was supposed to be lucky, or unlucky. I could never remember which.

He hefted it up as he swore. Nobody ever swore in our house. Not even a bugger, bum or sod. It just didn't happen. What's more Grandma was there. But Geoff swore at the top of his voice, shaking with passion. **"For fuck's sake, it's fucking Christmas and all you can**

fucking do is fucking argue about fucking fuck all ... it's driving me up the fucking wall." And with that, he hurled the, in this case the 'not lucky' Chinese temple dog across the room. It bounced heavily and just the once. He then rushed out of the living room, down the hall and out of the house. The front door slamming in his wake.

There was a stunned 30 second silence. It was as though a bomb had gone off. We were shocked and open mouthed. Then without missing a beat my mother said, "Jim, are you going to let him speak to me like that?"
And she was off again. This time with a renewed purpose.

I was so impressed by Geoff that day. In my eyes he was a lion dressed in a man's suit.

It wasn't the only time he impressed me but then all it takes is conviction. If someone says something to me and mean it down to their boots. That does it for me. I'm a sucker for that kind of certainty.

It was breakfast one Sunday morning and Geoff was already tucking into his.

"Do you want mushrooms with yours Ken?" my mother asked. "No thanks Mum, I don't like them" I said. My brother looked up and looked me straight in the eye and said "Ken, you don't know what you're missing. The world would be a sadder place without the mushroom". And that was it, he then just went back to his breakfast.

He said it with such conviction that I felt I was in the presence of wisdom. It has to be said that Geoff had never been the philosophical type. He had never said anything nearing profound before. Apart for the 'fucking fuck' incident. Which was more bold than profound. I never forgot this moment. Twenty years later Geoff became a mushroom farmer. I wasn't at all surprised. I thought it was destiny.

Christmas was always vaguely surreal. It was no different when I was much older. They'd retired and I went to visit them for Christmas at their bungalow on the Isle of Sheppey. What a bungalow it was. It was my mother's domain and my father's handiwork. On reflection that's how things had always been.

There was no 'adios nick knacks' here. This was knick-knack heaven. There wasn't a shelf unfilled. There wasn't an exposed piece of wood that couldn't be improved by a beaded edge or a bright coat of paint of unexpected hew. Say a pink or a yellow. Or be covered in floral patterned sticky backed paper. The walls, the shelves, the window-sills and the cupboards were covered in all manner of fine things. As well as cheap and cheesy tat. There was absolutely no discrimination whatsoever.

There were China plates with Dickensian scenes, American Indian heads in silhouette, toby jugs, novelty ash trays, tribes of figurines, brass plates, dishes, bowls, kettles a warming pan, a brass blow torch, a brass artillery casing with the fire tongs and poker in it. There were artificial flowers lovingly sprayed with just a hint from one of my mother's limited perfume range, African Violets or Lilly of the Valley.

There was a minimum of twelve different colored rugs in the living room. There were geraniums everywhere. There were geraniums on sills and on shelves. In hanging baskets and in china carts being pulled by donkeys. There were always geraniums. Last but by no means least there was the four- foot high 'Jeeves'

butler that always stood next to my mother's chair. He was made from wood in silhouette (my Dad's creation).
He was slightly bent at the waist, leaning forward hands outstretched, to permanently offer up the service of the brass ash tray, that was plugged into his clasped hands.

This was the bungalow. Well, there we were, it was Christmas Day. We'd had Christmas dinner. My mother and father were sound asleep, slumped in their chairs. Still with their paper Christmas cracker hats on. Which were all askew and sliding down the side of their heads, squashed against the wing of the high-backed armchairs.

I was slumped in a chair too, thinking there must be more to life than this. Rex, the dog, was asleep by the fire. It is worth mentioning that Rex was a cocker spaniel and not the brightest of dogs. We'd had a cocker spaniel when I was a boy. Now, he was clever, and he was also called Rex.

 This was a trait of my mother's, that I never quite figured out. Perhaps it saved on mental energy? Why waste time on trying to remember a different name.

She had probably half a dozen or more budgies during her lifetime. They were all called Jimmy. Every one of them. Dad was a Jim as well which was a bit spooky. I sometimes wondered if my father died, and she remarried, would the new man have to be called Jim also?

Not all the dogs were Rex's though. A few years later, after this Christmas, they inherited a Jack Russell. His name was Dougal. Dougal was fiercely intelligent, and fearless. His whole body would shake with suppressed energy. Dougal was a canine Loki.
It was this energy and focus that drove him to climb up onto the wing of one of the high- backed armchairs, and launch himself off, just as the budgie, 'Jimmy,' was sweeping past on one of his morning flights. He was let out of his cage to fly across the living room from shelf to shelf and pelmet to pelmet. That's when Dougal struck. He'd obviously been working it out for some time, from the low plains of the living room. This was no unhappy accident. This was a carefully considered plan.
Anyway, he leapt, and in one perfect arc, he caught Jimmy in his jaws .mid-flight. There was one startled squawk. Dougal landed noisily on the kitchen floor and

was out through the open door, into the garden, before you could say 'goodbye Jimmy'.

I wasn't there for this event. My mother told me about it over the phone. She'd been sat in the other high backed wing chair when this circus of horror had taken place. She was concerned but not unduly upset. She was rather entertained by it all. What a clever little rascal Dougal was. She admired him. She was a clever little rascal too. They were one of a kind. Anyway, you could always get another Jimmy.

So, there I was, Christmas afternoon bored and listless. Rex was asleep laying as close as possible to the Rayburn coal fire. His front paws and his head on the hearth. On one side of him was the brass coal bucket, with a small coal shovel balanced on it's top. It's handle hanging over the edge of the bucket. The shovel was overflowing with discarded walnut shells.

To the other side of Rex, my mother was slumped in her chair. Also close to the fire, with her cup of tea on the floor next to her. She was never ever too far from a cup of tea. As I watched the fire and listened to the six different clocks ticking, a small piece of hot coal spat out of the fire and hit the dog on the end of his nose. He leapt up with a startled yelp and shuffled backwards. Perplexed and confused. His back legs were either side of my mother's cup of tea. He went to settle himself down slowly as the heat of the spark had dissipated. As he lowered himself, his balls dipped straight into the cup of still hot tea. I'd never seen a look of astonishment on a dog's face before. He yelped, much louder this time, and leapt forward. His paws caught the end of the coal shovel, which flicked up with a force, firing shells round the room, some hitting my mother and father.

They both woke up with a splutter. "What's going on?", my mother asked. "I don't know where to start", I replied. At which point my mother leant over the side of her chair. In one fluid motion she picked up the teacup and saucer, took a sip of tea, and said "Oh well, at least my tea is still warm. Anything on the telly Jim?".

That night when I went to bed, I passed by the back of my father's chair. There was still a walnut shell lodged down the side of the Christmas hat that he was

wearing. I said goodnight and left them
to it.

Dad

My father was a magical man in so many ways. He was a member of the 'Magic Circle' and would entertain us at Christmas, and always at my birthday parties.
He was very good at it. On rare occasions though a trick would go wrong and there were repercussions.

On the day of my eighth birthday party. There was a mixed bag of six or seven school friends in the living room, and a few mums out in the dining room. Dad had set up his magic table and was in full flight. We sat around in a semi-circle riveted as he produced an omelette in an empty frying pan on a little calor gas stove, simply by waving his wand and making us shout Shim-Shala -Bim. Paper flowers came out of his magic wand. He pulled razor blades out of his mouth that had magically joined together on a string. It was great.

But then it happened. It seemed a simple enough trick by comparison. 'The magic Funnel.' He showed us the metal funnel. We looked through it to see that it was free of obstruction. He poured a pint of milk through it into a bowl to prove it.

Years later when I trawled through his magic paraphernalia in the attic. I realised the secret of many of the magic tricks, were often concealed in the mechanics of the equipment. I found the funnel and figured out that it had a secret chamber. If you twisted the spout of the funnel, it closed the tube and sent whatever liquid you poured into it, into the chamber.

On the day of the party after the demonstrations, he selected Sally, a winsome little girl, as his volunteer. He carefully placed the funnel under the elasticated waist at the top of her skirt. There were squawks of glee form the boys and gasps of horror from the girls. He must have twisted the tube too far, it had closed and then opened again. With a dramatic flourish he poured the bottle of milk into the funnel. We all gasped with surprise when we heard Sally squeak.
Then we saw the gush of milk as it appeared out of the bottom of her skirt and ran down her skinny pink legs.
Then she wailed. There was pandemonium. Mothers came rushing in. My father tried to placate her and them. He looked forlornly at the defective

funnel. Desperately trying to explain something that none of the gimlet-eyed women wanted to hear.

Needless to say, the party broke up after that. Sally's mum and dad didn't talk to us for a while. Oddly enough, of all the times I saw him do his impressive magic act. This is the day I remember the most.

He was magic in other ways. He was magic in the way that he loved me, and he let me know. He didn't say it, but he let me know. I knew he loved me. I knew, in the same way that I could feel the earth beneath my feet, and I could see the sun in the sky.

He loved me in the little gifts and presents he brought me.

Especially the 'magic pencil'

I was seven or eight when he gave me the pencil. It was in a tubular blue plastic case with a screw end about two to three inches long. Boys like that sort of cylindrical special purpose kind of thing. Inside was a small red pencil that was wrapped in a torn, weathered and distressed note. Like a pirate's map. When I unrolled the note, I saw it was written in a gothic script style. It said, "this is a magic pencil, whatever you write with this pencil will come true, but you must only use it for things that you really want."

It was wonderful. The times I would take it out of the container, read the note and carefully roll it up and put it away again. Just happy to have it, just in case.

He was a very calm man most of the time. I suppose he had to be. He was the ying to my mother's yang. He smoked a pipe. It was his worry beads. He would be constantly fiddling with it in a purposeful way. Cleaning it out, filling it up and tamping it down. Lighting it at practiced angles. Sucking on it to start the fire. Looking satisfied and blowing out smoke rings. Or he would be completely engrossed in some task and it was there in his mouth, in his hand or just a reach away.

I loved him completely, and still do.

Sex

Sex was never ever spoken about in our house, but in a way it was everywhere. It was in the electric charge in the kitchen the day my father said he'd drown the kittens and my mother scoffed. It was there in the games they played and the way they would taunt one another to go just that bit further.

It was there in their spontaneity. Getting my brother and I up out of bed one balmy August evening so that we could sleep in the garden, because it was such a beautiful warm night. My father insisting on showing us how you could sleep in a tree. My mother saying, "Oh get down Jim" but meaning "go on Jim, go higher, go higher".

The way he spent ages hiding behind doors and curtains, waiting for her to come along, so that he could just have her scream in surprise.

Although it was implicit everywhere, it was openly nowhere.
On my mother's part there was a lot of ignorance. There was no knowledge to pass on apart from the trauma of ignorance. She told me how when she first got married, she thought that you got pregnant through kissing.

She told me this story, time and time again, but it never occurred to her to tell my anything more than this or how you did get pregnant.

One day I came home from school, and she was over nice, "Sit down Ken, have a cup of tea Ken. Let's have another cup of tea Ken". I could tell something was up and it needed two cups of tea to be broached.

Then it dawned on me, she was going to talk to me about sex. That's why she was so uncomfortable. But I was wrong. She proceeded to tell me all that she knew about periods. She explained that no one had ever told her anything about periods. "When if first happened to me I thought I was bleeding to death Ken, I really did."
She didn't want me to be ignorant and not know about it.

There was a strange logic at work here. I left the room more confused than when I went in. What did this mean? Should I pass on this knowledge to my school friend's. Perhaps not.

The ignorance of all things sexual was quite amazing. Even after years of active married life it would still trip her up. It wasn't until she was in her eighties and Dad had long since died that she came anywhere close to speaking about sex. She'd voraciously taken up reading. That was her, all or nothing. She'd never read books much and then took it up enthusiastically at the age of 70. She read everything and anything. She went through a phase of reading Mills & Boon 'she clutched hungrily at his manhood' books.

"I've got to a really juicy bit in this one", she would say waving her copy of "The Married Lovers" at Geoff and I. Ever generous about sharing her latest obsession.
"I'm saving this for tonight", she would say, "I'm taking it to bed to read tonight with a packet of extra strong mints. I have to suck on a couple of extra strong mints otherwise I get overexcited".

Geoff was always a bit uncomfortable with all this. The revelation that our mother was a sexual being. And not only that but a sexual being in her seventies." I've never known anything like it you know, the things they get up to in these books". "Mind you", she'd say with a smile, "your dad was a bit of a one you know. You never knew what he'd get up to next, particularly on a Thursday night for some reason." She'd get a vaguely dreamy look on her face and Geoff would just have to leave the room.

So, she obviously wasn't unexperienced. But it all must have come as a complete surprise to her given her lack of knowledge in the first place. Maybe that was a bit of a challenge to my father. It was all another game, an opportunity to play.

I guess I'll never know. What I did see though were these occasional flashes of my mother's complete ignorance of some of the basics.

One time I arrived home from school to find her distraught in the kitchen. Every important event seemed to happen in the kitchen.
She was crying and making tea like there was a war on. "What's the matter Mum?", I asked. "Oh, Ken" she sobbed, "I can't tell you, I can't tell you. I never thought he would do anything like this to me". Anything like what, I thought, knowing he must be my father. "Do anything like what Mum, what's going on?", I persisted. "I just can't tell you Ken, you're too young" she sobbed. "I've rung him. I've rung him at work. You know I never ring him at work. I said if he didn't come home straight away, I was leaving. I didn't tell him why, but I made it clear if he didn't get home I was leaving". Blimey, I thought, this is serious and what the hell was it.........

I made more tea, intrigued and worried in equal doses and tried to tease it out of her. "Please mum, just calm down and tell me what's going on". "I can't Ken, I can't,

"Look mum, you've got to tell me", I said. She steeled herself. "We'll" she said rising from the table, "your dad went off to work this morning and he left his briefcase. I didn't want to let his sandwiches go to waste so I opened the briefcase". She picked up the briefcase "I found these". She dramatically tossed a handful of rubber finger stools onto the table.

I was open mouthed. She reached a pitch of anguish, "He never uses these things with me, he must have another woman", she wailed. Then I got it. She thought these finger stools, that my sister, a hairdresser, had given my father to wear to protect a cut finger, were 'Condoms'…. She'd never seen a condom. As we spoke my father was rushing home from London because she was leaving him, and he had absolutely no clue as to why.

I laughed. Mum was shocked. This wasn't the reaction she'd been expecting at all. "Ken", how can you laugh at a time like this?" She slumped back down into the chair. Once I'd calmed her down, I explained to her what they were, where my father had got them and why.

"Oh dear", she said, "so there not…….. (she couldn't say the words condoms)? "No", I said, shaking my head. "Oh dear", she repeated, "and your dads on his way home.

He turned up, wild eyed and anxious. He burst through the front door, down the hallway into the kitchen. "What on earth is going on

Maud?". I left them to it. Happy days.

This lack of basic knowledge of the mechanics of all things sexual was effectively passed down to me. They told me all they knew, which was absolutely nothing, apart from the traumas you experience with your first period. The boys in the playground at school were adamant that you made babies by weeing into girls. Maybe they were right. Who knew?

So, when my Dutch rabbits had their first litter. Which were boys and which were girls? I didn't know, dad didn't know, and my mother certainly didn't. As ever though, she knew someone who did. Judy Fagen. Judy lived a few so doors away. "Judy's been breeding rabbits for years.", Said mum. I was sent off with a box full of baby rabbits to knock on Mrs. Fagen's door. What do I say to her mother? I worried. "Excuse me Mrs Fagen but could Judy sex my rabbits?". It's worth saying that Judy was bout my age but going on eighteen. To my surprise, it was Judy who answered the door. She was dressed in a fluffy white dressing gown, with a towel on her head, straight from the shower. I mumbled and managed to ask her. She smiled that smile, that women have, when they know they're totally in control of the situation.
"I can do it", she said, "come in it won't take a minute". We sat in her front room as she, without hesitation, picked up each rabbit with a

firm hand, turned it over, glanced between it's legs and said, 'boy' or 'girl'. All the time looking straight at me. I was hugely impressed and electrified by the glimpse of soft thigh as her dressing gown parted slightly. I knew I was totally out of my depth here.

Everything about her, her confidence, the twinkle in her eye, the way she handled the rabbits, said that in the sex stakes, we just were not in the same league.

She smiled as I mumbled my thanks. As I left and she stood looking stunning at the front door, and said, "If you have any trouble Ken, you can come back any time".

"Thanks", I said wishing that I could go back, and she could turn me over with those deft hands, and sought me out, boy or man?

I didn't go back, but the vision of her with her hair in the towel standing at the doorstep still lives on in me.
The other image that never leaves, me and was really at the start of my sexual awakening, happened before I knew that I didn't know anything. It was also my mother's doing really.

We went on holiday for a while, every summer, to Broadstairs. Mum, Dad, Geoff, me and Grandma. Down on the train, a 'nice' B & B and our own chalet on the beach. Long days of clammy woollen swimming trunks. In and out of the sea, which sometimes went out for miles. We'd trudge through the muddy pools and poke the dead jellyfish with sticks. My Grandmother always in a bonnet, a cardigan and thick, tea- coloured stockings. Cricket on the beach, ice creams and fun. There's still a photograph about of me buried in the sand up to my neck with a bucket on my head. One of the highlights of the week was the theatre by the pier. Friday night was family night. We'd all be there singing "Bobbing up and down like this" and "All the nice girls love a sailor", it was great, I absolutely loved it. With the odd exception. They always had a raffle with 5 or 6 winners. If you won you had to go up on the stage and give your ticket to the M.C, who would give you your prize, then everyone applauded. One evening during the raffle he called out number twelve (12). We had ticket number one hundred and twenty-two (122). Without a moment's hesitation my mother tore the last two (2) off the strip. She gave me the remainder, shot her hand up in the air and yelled "winner." Then she said "Ken, take this up there". "But it's not the right ticket Mum", I said, "I don't want to go". "Just do it", she said in that tone that meant there was no arguing, so I trudged up to the stage to wild applause. "What have we here" said e M.C. gleefully. "This young fellow has torn the end of his ticket to make it look like a winner. What shall we do? give him a prize for his cheek or send him packing?". They cheered and booed in equal doses. I was mortified, he gave me a prize. I can't remember what it was, I didn't care. My mother of course was delighted.

They also used to have a talent contest for the kids and three or four kids would volunteer and do a turn. The M.C. would pick a winner from the audience's response. I can't remember much about the turns now apart from this one single occasion that is branded forever into my memory. It was the slot in the show for the talent contest and my mother turned to me and said, "Go on Ken, go and do that song you know". It was 'I've never felt more like singing the blues.

A popular song at the time. Well, I did not want to go on that stage or any stage and sing "I've never felt more like singing the blues". It was bad enough having to sing it in the living room surrounded by various aunts and uncles. "I don't want to Mum" I said, but she had that look in her eyes and there was no getting out of it. I resisted, she insisted. So off I trudged up to the stage again.
"What's your name son?" said the M.C. over the mike, "and he's going to sing etc. etc". I had to queue up with the hopefuls in the wings. One by one we moved nearer the stage, before entering to stand in the dazzle of the spotlight. There was no talking. I was terrified. Everyone

seemed excited or skittish, except for the girl in front of me. She was a few years older than me, maybe thirteen. There was a palpable calm about her. She stood perfectly still, slightly up on her toes. Poised and focussed like a delicate, but powerful animal. She fascinated me. We moved ever closer to the stage until there was just her and I standing in the wings. It was strangely intimate. We didn't know one another, we didn't speak. But we were both going to jump out of the plane. Then, her turn came. The M.C. called out her name. I can't remember it. She strode confidentially across the stage and in one fluid motion, lifted her skirt, tucked into the elastic top of her knickers, flipped over into a perfect handstand.

She sang, "Maybe it's because I'm a Londoner". There was a slight trembling of her thighs.

I was mesmerised. Something about her confidence, the exposed thighs, her knickers and the upside downness of it. It all combined into an exotic cocktail. I felt something I had never felt before. I didn't know what it was, but I liked it.

Although I'd not been told anything about sex, what had been drummed into me though, was that you must not get anybody pregnant. That was taboo. Unacceptable.

I was 19 when Carole, my first real girlfriend, told me she was pregnant. This is it I thought. How can I tell them? It's a disaster. They will disown me.

I finally plucked up the courage. I was fully expecting to be told to leave. We sat in the living room. I told them. They were quiet. I hung my head.

Then they said "What do you and Carole want to do?

Do you want to have the baby? It's your life. We will support you both, whatever you choose" And they did. They were fantastic. I was completely knocked out by their open-hearted love and support. It was a game changer. The whole thing became something good and positive. Something to celebrate. Lisa, our daughter was born, loved by Carole and I, and equally loved by my mother and father.

Once Carole went back to work mum took Lisa to nursery and school. It gave my mother a new lease of life. Dad taught her songs. She became an integral part of their lives.

Roll on 12 years and Carole and I had drifted apart. Perhaps we were too young? Anyway, after a year of trying to work it out, but failing, I decided I had to leave.

I went to see mum and dad to tell them. They had retired by now.

We had a cup of tea, of course, and I told

them. My mother looked shocked. "But ken"
she said" you can't be leaving you've only just
fitted a new bathroom suite!"
It was true,
I had only recently had a new bathroom suite
installed. I must be mad.

Life moved on and later I met 'the lovely Pat.' It
was difficult to start a new relationship as I was
still trying to come to terms with the guilt and
sadness of the separation. But I knew she was
the ONE. This was it. The magic my mother
had talked about had happened to me. This
was my kiss under the mistletoe experience.
Once Pat and I were getting serious I took her
to meet mum and dad. She was nervous.
When it was time to leave my mother took Pat
by the hands, looked her in the eye, smiled and
said" You two would make lovely babies."
And we did. We made Lucy and Jamie.

Waving Goodbye

My mother talked about her death quite regularly. "When I go Ken", she'd say during one of our intimate moments. Her in her favourite armchair, with a cup of tea, relaxed and thoughtful. "I'd like everyone to sing 'Wish me luck as you wave me goodbye.' Not one of those boring hymns." She'd sing a bit of it just to make sure I got the point and realised what a good idea it was. Or she would say 'Horses', that's what I'd like, horses. Everyone would stop to look. The horses could do their business in the road and people could collect if up afterwards for their gardens".

As a child this kind of talk used to worry me quite a bit, I was uncomfortable with it. I didn't want to be left alone. As time went on though I became used to it, it was a familiar mantra of hers and I could tell she got pleasure out of watching us squirm. I say us because all the family were made to suffer this conversation. There was no exception.
My father would tut and splutter and say the requisite "Oh don't be silly Maud".
My sister would get annoyed, my brother would look sad and tearful. I was the only one who, to start with, just listened.

I had no choice, but as time went on I would join in. We would create elaborate plans with gleaming coaches and black horses and hosts of weeping, no sobbing, mourners. She loved it. It was a good game.

Eventually, of course, as the years rolled on, she got nearer and nearer to it being a reality. She was in her late eighties and frail and coming to the end of the road. We would still have enthusiastic conversations about the arrangements. It was just the details that changed and thankfully it scaled down from the Victorian Gothic creation that it had once been. The one thing she insisted on was that we played' Wish me luck as you wave me goodbye' as the coffin disappeared.

She was in hospital. It was just after a Christmas. She was just weak and old really. My sister called me on a Thursday night and said that this might be it. That mum was on her last legs and that if we wanted to say our goodbyes, now was the time.

I took the next day off work and drove

down to the hospital in Chatham to see her. I deliberately went on my own and realised that this might be my last visit. I was determined to be positive about it. I was sad but calm. I knew there was absolutely no unresolved business between us. Not one thing.

I knew her inside out. I'd seen her at her best and at her worst. I loved her. I loved all of her. The whole complex difficult, desperate, wicked and wonderful package. And she knew it.

Once when she was in her seventies and I was in my thirties I was visiting her in her sheltered flat in Norfolk. We were sitting alone, with a cup of tea, like so many times before. She looked at me and said, "I'm sorry Ken." I said, "Sorry for what, Mum?".
"You know when you were younger when I would get depressed and have to go away. It must have been awful for you?". She'd never said anything like this before. I know she'd felt guilty at the time because she used to come out of hospital, 'back to normal' and I'd get a new bike or a Davy Crocket hat or best of all, a dog, Rex.

I saw that day, that she still carried it

with her. Although she thought I'd accepted it all and didn't blame her, she wasn't sure. She was prepared to face it out and take whatever I had to say. This was my moment to unload.

I looked her straight in those clever blue eyes and said, "Mum, you haven't got to be sorry. What happened was what happened. It's life and it's made me who I am." I meant it and it felt good to say it. It felt good to see the relief and love in her eyes. We moved on to another subject and a bit later had a bit of a sing song.

When I found her in the hospital ward it was a bit of a shock. There was this crumpled rag doll asleep in the bed. It looked like the life was already leaking out of her and she'd shrunk down to mere skin and bone. I steadied myself, sat down, took her hand and talked to her as she slept. Eventually she stirred, came around and half sat up. She was confused and didn't really know who I was. I stuck with it and she began to talk, which was an effort. The more she talked the more alive she became. The effort of it seemed to make her grow a bit larger. Like air entering into a deflated balloon. As she talked the more with it she became, "I'm still not sure who you are," she said," but I like you".

I helped her sit up in the bed and she became more coherent. She began reminiscing about my father, how he loved me and what a good son I'd been. Then she asked about my family, were the children well and all of that. She lent towards me, "because your health Ken, that's what counts.
Not money and status and all of that. None of that matters. Money Ken, you can't take it with you when you go".
"Your right Mum", I responded. She beckoned me closer to her and she said conspiratorially "mind you I'm taking something with me when I go." She glanced around the ward to make sure no one was listening. "Are you Mum?", I said, "Yes", she said, "Do you want to know what it is?", "yes Mum", I said, "What is it?".

There was a pause for dramatic effect. **"Tea Bags",** she exclaimed, delighted at the look on my face. Her eyes sparkled, she burst out laughing and so did I.
She'd got me. The old devil. It was another game. We both laughed enjoying the moment.

I drove back to London with a warm glow. I thought that if that was my last conversation with my mum, I couldn't ask for more. It wasn't our last conversation though. She rallied and a week later was out of the hospital. She lived for another two years.

I'm sure it was that spirit in her, that sense of fun and mischief that kept her going. That spirit that had brought her back from all those little deaths in the black days of her depression. She was a brave and remarkable woman. An inspiration.

My dad died in his mid- seventy's way before her. "I do miss my Jim" she would often say. He died too early and completely unexpectedly. He'd just met Pat and could see we were happy. He never met our children, Lucy and Jamie, which was a real shame. He would have loved them, and they would have loved him.

My brother Geoff also died unexpectedly. Too soon and too young. We did spend some time with him together as a family and he got to know and love Lucy and Jamie.

My sister, June, asked me to move her

into a care home near us after her partner, Stan, had died. So, I did. She was happy there. Safe and well looked after.

I could call in and see her once or twice a week. I had three great years of being able to see her regularly and enjoy her beauty, charm and humour, before she finally slipped away.

But then there was new life. Lisa had moved to Australia with husband Karl and my grandsons', Jake and Taylor. And in time along came my great grandson Finley.

In more recent years Lucy met Dan and Jamie met Lily. The family and the love has grown. And so, it goes.

Finale

Life with Maud has taught me:

Make the most of it, all of it.
Make the most of your family and
friends.
A sense of humour is essential.
Be ready to play.
Look for the best in people.
The more you are who you are the more
people love you.
The people we love live on in us and the
stories we tell of them.

THE END

Life With Maud

Appendix 1

Life With Maud

Appendix 2

Inside Out Show Script

Note: This script, performed at an Inside
Out Show, was based directly on Maud's
character and included some things she
had actually said.

-Home Visits

Old woman: Mrs Wainright
Nurse: Carol Smith
Daughter: Sandra

CURTAINS OPEN

Old woman at table reading mills and boon novel

There is a ring at the doorbell

OW: Who is it?

N: it's the district nurse…Carol

OW: O come in then…….Sit down love. Who are you again ?

N: Carol Smith , the district nurse, I heard you had been poorly, so I popped by.

OW: About bloody time too….I could be dead or worse here …don't see anyone from one day to the next …as for family well …I don't know why I bothered to be honest

N: it must be hard for you Mrs Wainwright …how are you feeling generally?

OW: oh not so bad really….I have good days and bad days…I'm sure there must be a lot more worse off than me …….look at that Princess Diana…gone just like that
(shakes her head ruefully) all that exercise for nothing. Then there's that Jordan girl…she's had

breast implants left right and centre and she still can't hang on to a man...

N: You're ok then Mrs. Wainwright ?

OW: I do get a bit lonely ...I miss my Jim

N: Jim was your husband?

OW: Yeh... there's not a day goes by when I don't think of him you know.

N: (picks up framed photo) Is this him?

OW: Yeh.. that's my Jim

N: He looks very nice

OW; He were a lovely man... every one said so ..... I think about him all the time you know...only this morning they played a song on the radio from that Phantom of the Opera.....I remember him taking to see that at Covent Garden...it was one of our first dates.

N: Really that must have been wonderful

OW: Not really love...some bloke bent over his organ with half his face missing...not my cup of tea really

N: Oh right

OW: our honeymoon though that was lovely.... I was so scared I thought if a man kissed you you'd get pregnant...that's how things were in those days

N: Really?...were you virgo intacto then?

OW: No we stayed in a small B&B in Broadstairs

N: (just opens mouth)

(there is a ring at the door bell and a voice calls out)

D: Hello ....mum ...it's me ...anybody there?

(OW looks furtive wraps shawl around her starts moaning the nurse looks perplexed....enter daughter)

D: Mum it's me.....(sees Nurse) ....oh hello

N: I'm Carol the district nurse

D: oh dear Mum are you ill ...is she ill?

OW: (acting feeble etc) : is there somebody there?

D: (taking her hand) Mum it's me are you ok?

OW: (feeble and pathetic) Who are you ...do I know you?

D: It's me Shirley your daughter...

OW: daughter ...daughter ......I don't have a daughter do I?...aren't they people that come round and see you all the time and call you on the telephone to see how you are....I'm sure I haven't got one of those.

D: (falls in and sits up) Oh please don't do all this mum...I'm here now aren't I?

OW (sitting up as normal etc) And about bloody time too I could have bee dead or worse for all you knew .

D: That's not true and you know it and anyway now I am here now let's make the most of it shall we? .

N: I'll get going then.

OW: No dear you stay besides you haven't had a cup of tea yet.

N: (looking at D)Well if you're both sure .

OW: Look it's my bloody house not hers...yet.....it's up to me who stays and who goes.

D: All right mum

OW: I'll give you all right mum...I suppose you want a cup of tea too.

D: That would be nice thank you

OW: (mocking) That would be nice thank you......Right I'll get the tea then.

D: I'll do it if you like.

OW: No no I can do it...you just stay there.... then you can both talk about me when I've gone

D: what ever you say.

(the old woman rises and shuffles off there is a ripple of fart as she exits)

D: (embarrassed to N) I'm sorry about that .
N: Don't worry ..they all get a bit like that.
D: No I meant...the wind..
N: So did I

(OW returns with tray of teas)

OW: Right.....chocolate finger anybody??

CURTAIN.

Printed in Dunstable, United Kingdom